INSCRIBED FOR SUE MARCH
WITH KINDEST WISHES
2/2/75

Etchings of ISRAEL
LAND of the BIBLE

No 380 of A Limited Edition

Alec
Stern

ETCHINGS OF ISRAEL
LAND OF THE BIBLE

STUDIO EDITION

PUBLISHED BY STUDIO OF ALEC STERN

SAN MATEO, CALIFORNIA

© ALEC STERN 1974

INTRODUCTION

Israel! The Holy Land! The Land of the Bible! By whatever name she is called, what visions these familiar words conjure up, what hopes they instill in the faithful!

The Christian pictures Jesus, Bethlehem, the Sea of Galilee, Nazareth, the Via Dolorosa, the Holy Sepulchre. . . .

The Jew envisions Jerusalem the Golden, her holy Western Wall with memories of the Temple, Mt. Zion, King David, Rachel's Tomb. . . .

The Moslem sees the Dome of the Rock, Mohammed, Mt. Moriah.

Israel, the land of the Bible! Although I had never thought of myself as a religious person, when I arrived in Jerusalem for the first time in 1966, I felt her spirituality deeply and began to understand her powerful attraction to people of the various faiths. I had intended to stay but two weeks and prepare a few sketches, but, as the days passed, became aware that I was in a vast treasure house of antiquities and must remain longer.

So my wife and I rented a car and drove through the land of the prophets for two months, from Haifa and the Sea of Galilee in the north to the ancient seaport of Jaffa and inland again to Jerusalem, then south through the Negev to Beersheba and Sodom to King Solomon's Mines and Eilat on the Red Sea.

The accomplishments of our people in a few short years after nearly 2000 years of dispersion overwhelmed us. Modern communities with Biblical names springing up where ancient cities once stood, homes and factories being constructed in the desert, forests being planted on denuded hills where trees had flourished before the Crusaders and the Turks—Israeli energy seemed inexhaustible.

El Al Airlines had commissioned me to prepare a few sketches, but the few grew to many. Upon my return home I planned to produce a small booklet of them, but as I continued to add more and more subjects related to the three great religions, the collection seemed incomplete without quotations from the Scriptures, and so for the first time in my life I found myself reading the Bible seriously while searching for passages appropriate to each of the etchings. From the quotations grew additional research in preparing the descriptive text accompanying each subject. A second trip to Israel produced more etchings. Before realizing it, I had in my hands a full-fledged book, which we have produced in our studio on our own presses.

I hope you will get the same joy out of it as I have in creating it.

Cordially,

Alec Stern

CONTENTS

ETCHINGS WITH ACCOMPANYING SCRIPTURES
AND DESCRIPTIVE TEXTS

THIS BOOK

And thou shall make a candlestick of pure gold: of beaten work shall the candlestick be made: even its base and its shaft ... and there shall be six branches going out of the sides thereof; three branches out of one side thereof ... and three branches out of the other side .... and thou shalt make the lamps thereof, to give light over against it.

Exodus 25

MENORAH - Symbol of Light

A seven branched Candelabra occupied a prominent place in the temples of early Judea. It is found on both their ancient coins and those of today and has become the emblem of the State of Israel. This magnificent bronze menorah, sculptured by B. Elkan, was the gift of the British Government to Israel's Parliment in 1948 as a token of their esteem. It stands sixteen feet high and is enhanced with figures in relief depicting great events in Jewish history.

Pray for the peace
of Jerusalem;
    they shall prosper
that love Thee.
    Peace be within
thy walls, and prosper-
ity within thy palaces.

Psalms 122

The OLD CITY of JERUSALEM

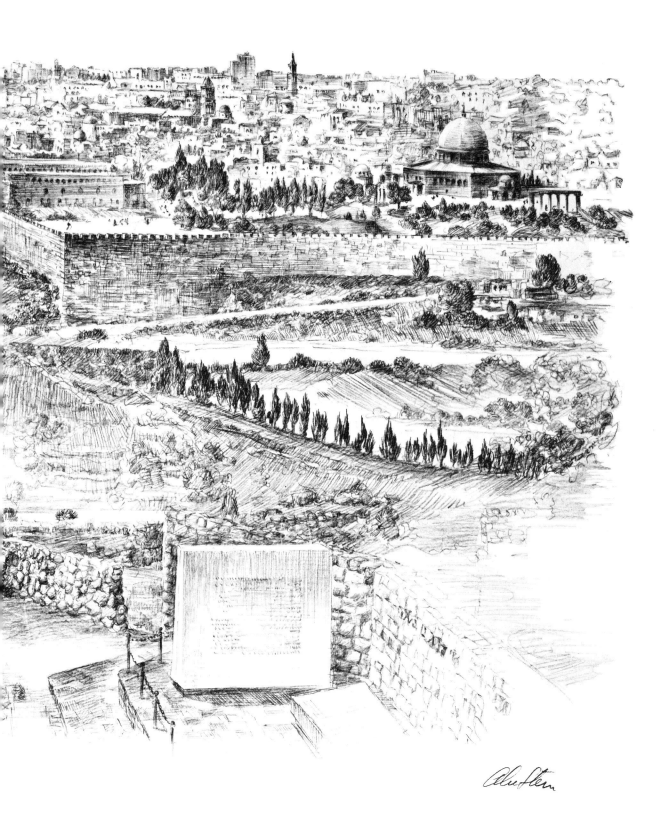

13

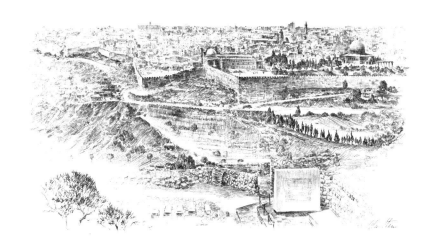

The Holy City of JERUSALEM
One of the oldest cities in the world, Jerusalem the Golden! Archeol-
ogists have found reference to her written on clay tablets four thousand
years old. Within its ancient walls one is transported into a world
of antiquity where with a little imagination the Bible comes to life ~
historical shrines of the great faiths, oriental bazaars, exotic foods and
a myriad of other attractions including musical and mystical.

Greater love hath
no man than this,
that a man lay
down his life for his
friends ~~~ These things
I command you, that
ye love one another ~

St. John 15

VIA DOLOROSA

Traditionally accepted as the winding street of the fourteen stations that Jesus followed from condemnation to crucifixion. The way is usually crowded with Christian pilgrims, white-robed Arabs, Israelis, Nuns, Priests and the clergy of other sects.

SIXTH STATION OF THE CROSS
Via Dolorosa

And it came to pass
in the four hundred
and eightieth year
after the children of Israel
came out of the land of
Egypt, in the fourth year
of Solomon's reign over
Israel, in the month of
Zif, ~~~ that he began to
build the house of the Lord~

1 Kings 6

The WESTERN WALL

The WESTERN WALL - One of the holiest shrines of
the Jewish people and symbol of their unity.

Nearly 2000 years of tragic memories are stored up in these weathered
blocks of stone, remnants of the magnificent Second Temple erected
by Herod the Great in Twenty B.C.E. and destroyed by the Romans
a century later. What calamities they must have witnessed during
the invasions by the armies of the Persians and Byzantines, Moslems
and Crusaders, Turks and others throughout the ages.

Oh Lord save thy people, the remnant of Israel." Behold, I will ...gather them from the lands of the earth, ...Then shall the virgin re-joice in the dance; both young men and old together; for I will turn their sorrow into joy..."

Jeremiah 31

DANCING AT THE WALL
Pious Jews and their brethren gather at the liberated Holy Wall with uninhibited expressions of joy and sorrow, elation, and meditation with religious fervor. Nineteen centuries of prayers have been answered. They are the fortunate generation chosen to witness this miracle.

Where Abraham made ready to sacrifice his only son to the glory of God... "Take now thy son, thine only son whom thou lovest, even Issac, and get thee into the land of Moriah; upon one of the mountains..."

Genesis 22

THE DOME of THE ROCK, Jerusalem

THE DOME of THE ROCK Jerusalem

MOSQUE of OMAR

Highlighting the exotic skyline of the Holy City is this gold-crowned jewel of Islamic architecture - The Dome of the Rock. Sheltered within its exquisite mosaic-covered walls lies the sacred rock atop Mount Mariah from whence, according to Moslem tradition, the prophet Mohammed ascended into heaven.

Behold I will take
the children of
Israel from among
the non-believers, whither
they be gone, ... into their
own land: and I will make
them into one nation, ...
and I will be their God.
And David my servant
shall be King over them

Ezekiel 37

DAVID'S TOWER

Adjacent to Jaffa Gate is one of Jerusalem's most important historical sites, the Citadel and its prominent tower. It was built by Herod the Great about twenty B.C.E. and spared by Titus when he destroyed The City ninety years later. Throughout the centuries the Citadel passed through many wars and was considered Jerusalem's strongest point of defense.

DAVIDS TOWER

For the Lord has
chosen Zion;
  He has longed
for it as a dwelling
place for Himself;
  "This is my resting
place forever;....."

Psalm 132

MT. ZION

MT. ZION

In ancient times Mt. Zion was within the walls of Jerusalem. Jew and Moslem revere it as the traditional site of David's grave and Christians as the scene of the last supper and Mary's death. The Memorial Tomb of David and the Cenacle are housed in one building; a statue of Mary in repose rests in a crypt in the Church of the Dorminton nearby.

Go ye into the city, there shall ye meet a man... and he will show you a large upper room furnished and prepared. And his disciples went forth, and came into the city, and found as he hath said unto them: and they made ready the passover.

Mark 14

HALL OF THE LAST SUPPER   The Coenaculum
Jesus and the disciples celebrated the first night of Passover in this
room. The worn stones of the floor are vivid proof of the uncount-
able numbers of pilgrims who have visited this holy shrine in the course
of centuries. The graceful pointed arches flaring out from the heavy
marble columns with their distinctively carved capitols clearly show
Crusader influence.

SITE OF THE LAST SUPPER
MT. ZION, ISRAEL

41

Now the rulers
of the people
lived in Jerusalem:
and the rest of the people
cast lots to bring one out
of ten to dwell in Jerusalem
the holy city, ...

Nehemiah 11

The KNESSET BUILDING

The KNESSET BUILDING

This impressive structure of Jerusalem's beautiful pink stone hugs the hilltop as though it were part of it. It is the home of the one hundred and twenty members of Parliament, the governing body of the State of Israel's democratic republic. Its public halls display superb tapestries and mosaics by Marc Chagall. Also exhibited are sculptures, paintings and other works by Israeli artists.

A woman of valor
who can find?
For her price is
above rubies. The heart
of her husband doth safely
trust her, and he hath no
lack of gain. ... She
stretcheth out her hand
to the poor; Yea, she
reacheth forth her hands
to the needy.

Proverbs 31

MOTHER and CHILD *Sculpture by Chaim Gross*
The joy of motherhood is eloquently portrayed by this sculpture of copper in the courtyard of the Mother and Child Pavilion of Hadassah Medical Center. Your artist came upon it while visiting his sick wife at the hospital, where in the emergency room he witnessed the busy staff's impartial treatment of Arabs and Jews. Before long they informed his wife, although they knew her to be an active Hahassah member, that she had sufficiently recovered to give up her bed to an injured Arab woman.

MOTHER and CHILD

49

Health and fit condition of body are above all gold, and a strong body above great wealth. There is no riches above a sound body~

Ecclesiastes 30

HADASSAH-HEBREW UNIVERSITY
MEDICAL CENTER

53

HADASSAH - HEBREW UNIVERSITY Medical Center
Above the village of Ein-Karem stands Hadassah Hospital, one of the most modern medical institutions in the world. It was the vision of Henrietta Szold, an American, who in 1912 formed a committee to alleviate suffering among the Palestinian Jews. This small group, now called 'Hadassah', has grown to an organization of three hundred and fifty thousand dedicated American-Jewish women. The Medical Center's services are available to all regardless of race, color or creed, without cost to those unable to pay.

An Angel appeared and saith to ∼∼∼ Zacharias ✛✛✛ "Thy prayer is heard and thy wife Elizabeth shall bear thee a son and thou shalt call his name John".

Luke 1

The CHURCH OF ST. JOHN THE BAPTIST
St. John the Baptist was born in a grotto in the ancient village of Ein-Karem. This biblical site just outside of Jerusalem nestles in a beautiful valley lush with vineyards and olive groves. The nine hundred year old church owned by the Franciscans is built above the grotto and contains numerous art treasures including early paintings and frescos.

Therefore all things whatsoever ye would that men should do to you do ye even so to them: for this is the law and the prophets.

St. Matthew 7

MONASTERY of THE CROSS

The MONASTERY of THE CROSS

According to Greek Orthodox tradition the wood for the Cross of
Christ was obtained from a tree growing on this site. The Monastery
is located in the Jerusalem corridor and was built by Georgian kings
of the Caucacus in the twelfth century. It was designed in the form
of a fortress as protection against bands of thieves.

Happy is the nation whose God is the Lord: The people whom he hath chosen for His own inheritance+ Our soul hath waited for the Lord; He is our help and our shield~ For in Him doth our heart rejoice, Because we have trusted in His Holy name~

Psalms 12

MEA-SHEARIM - Community of 100 Gates
This stronghold of Jewish Orthodoxy in the New City was founded
in 1877 by European Jews from the Old City. It is one of the most
colorful parts of Jerusalem, for the residents retain the life style of
the ghettos of Europe. They dress in the manner of that period,
wearing felt or fur hats, black alpaca coats, beards and sidelocks, the
women modestly dressed with their heads covered. Yiddish is the every-
day language, Hebrew being reserved for holy matters.

רחוב במאה שערים

A STREET IN MEA'-SHE'ARIM, Jerusalem

65

Who is wise?
He that learns
from all men ...

If there is no knowledge
there is no understanding;
If there is no understanding
there is no knowledge —

Mishnah 1-21

HEBREW UNIVERSITY
GIVAT RAM CAMPUS

69

HEBREW UNIVERSITY Givat Ram Campus
The renowned Hebrew University is located in the peaceful moun-
tainous landscape of Jerusalem. When the Jordanians cut off access
to the Mt. Scopus campus in nineteen forty-seven, plans for the
present Givat Ram campus started immediately. The facilities of the
new campus soon outstripped those of the old. When Mt. Scopus was
freed in nineteen sixty-seven, the activities of the two were united.

And he came and lived in a city called Nazareth: that it might be fulfilled which was spoken by the prophets He shall be called a Nazarene.

St. Matthew 3

A STREET IN NAZARETH

Ancient descriptions of Nazareth indicate that she still retains much of the charm of the period when Jesus lived here. While sketching this crooked little street your artist sensed a bit of the past and enjoyed the incongruity of the present; the bearded Arab astride a chugging motorcycle, the black-robed sister on a sluggish donkey; the odor of the meat stall, the fragrance of the flower stands; Moslem women with covered faces, modern women with little covering; the Jewish youth with a yamalkah atop his head buying halvah, speaking Arabic, two white-veiled Catholic nuns conversing in Hebrew - - - - - all just beautiful!

A STREET IN NAZARETH,
ISRAEL

73

His disciples saw
Jesus walking on
the sea, drawing
close to the ship, and
they were afraid, but
he sayeth unto them,
"It is I, be not afraid"

John 6

the SEA of GALILEE

SEA OF GALILEE ~ Lake Kinneret
The shoreline of this beautiful lake follows the graceful curves of a
harp, softened by lush growth of eucalyptus, palms and other semi-
tropical vegetation. The shepherds have tended their flocks here since
biblical days and the fishermen continue to haul in their silvery catches
over the centuries. The scene of Jesus' ministry brings pilgrims from
many lands. Its warm winters and mineral springs has attracted
health seeking vacationers and sportsmen since Roman times.

After leaving Nazareth, He came and took up residence in Capernaum, beside the sea ... Then He went around throughout the whole of Galilee teaching in their Synagogues ...

Matthew 4

The SYNOGOGUE of CAPERNAUM
One of the best known archeological sites of Israel is the partially
rebuilt ruins of this ancient synogogue in Capernaum near the
shores of the Sea of Galilee. The skillfully sculptured and well
preserved stones depict many facets of early Jewish culture. The
gospel tells us this was the home of and where the ministry of
Jesus began. The Franciscan fathers purchased the site in 1894
and did substantial restoration.

The Synogogue at Capernaum

Moreover the Lord said unto me, take thee a great roll, and write in it with a man's pen ...

Isaiah 4

The SHRINE of THE BOOK

Alw Stern

The SHRINE OF THE BOOK

Among the modern buildings that make up the Israel Museum complex is one with a brilliant white, onion shaped roof - The Shrine of The Book. Its unique roofline symbolizes the cover of a jar containing the Dead Sea Scrolls found in a cave near the Dead Sea. This still readable manuscript of the Book of Isaiah is on display in the shrine.

And seeing the
multitudes, He
went up into a moun-
tain, and when He had
set down His disciples
came unto Him ~~~ and
taught them, saying
"Blessed are the poor
in spirit, for theirs is
the kingdom of heaven~~
"Blessed are the meek,
for they shall inherit
the earth...

Matthew 5

CHURCH OF THE MOUNT OF BEATITUDES

The scriptures tell us that Jesus preached the famous 'Sermon on the Mount', the essence of Jesus' doctrine, and also chose the Apostles on the Mount of the Beatitudes. The white-trimmed church overlooking the peaceful Sea of Galilee is in the care of the Italian Franciscan Nuns. Imbedded in the floor surrounding the altar of the church are plaques symbolizing the seven virtues: Justice, Charity, Prudence, Faith, Fortitude, Temperance and Hope.

CHURCH OF THE TRANSFIGURATION
Mt. Tabor, Israel

Judges and officers
shalt thou make
thee in all thy gates
which the Lord thy God
giveth thee, and they
shall judge the people
with righteous judgment.
Justice, Justice shalt
thou follow that thou
mayest live, and inherit
the land which the Lord
thy God giveth thee.

Deuteronomy 18

HEIKHAL-SHLOMO *Solomon's Mansion*
This stately building of white stone in Jerusalem, built through a donation by Sir Isaac Walton . . . is the seat of the Chief Rabbinate of Israel and the Supreme Religious Centre where international Jewish Congresses are held. It houses a synagogue, a library and a museum containing three-dimensional models of great events in Jewish history as well as artifacts and historical documents.

Allahu akbar! Allah
is most great!
There is no God but
Allah! Mohammed is
Allah's Apostle! Pray
thou now, Pray thou now!
Come to salvation, Come
to salvation! Prayer is
more fruitful than sleep!
Prayer is more fruitful
than sleep! Allaho akhav!
Allah is most great!
There is no God but Allah

The Moslem call to prayer

THE GREAT MOSQUE OF ACRE
Within the massive Crusader walls of Acre stands an 18th century Mosque, one of the finest in Israel, called the Jazzer Mosque after its founder. Israel's Ministry of Religious Affairs reconditioned the structure for its Moslem congregation, who in turn reciprocated by keeping its doors open to all visitors. The facade is richly decorated with ornamental tile and the interior covered with handsome oriental rugs, and a sign reads, "Please remove your shoes upon entering".

The GREAT MOSQUE, Acre - Israel

97

Behold, how good and how pleasant it is for brethren to dwell together in unity! It is like the precious ointment upon the head, that ran down upon the beard... As the dew of Hermon, That cometh down upon the mountains of Zion; For there the Lord commanded the blessing, even life for ever.

Psalms 133

HAIFA - from MT. CARMEL

HAIFA

The eyes of the artist were drawn from the verdant pines and stately cedars atop Haifa's Mt. Carmel to the golden dome of the Baha'i shrine below. His vision continued down the slopes passing homes gardens clinging to the hillside, finally reaching the waterfront and the huge ornamental silo storing grain for shipment abroad. Alongside the quays the ships were busy with cargo, and beyond was the poet's blue Mediterranean. What a beautiful setting for a great industrial center!

The children of
Israel walked
forty years in
the wilderness ~~~
The Lord sware unto
their fathers that he
would give us a land
that floweth with milk
and honey ~~~

Joshua 5

CARMEL MARKET Tel Aviv
The Occident and the Orient meet in an exotic display of color,
enticing natives and tourists to Tel Aviv's open air market place.
Bright awnings and striped umbrellas cast their cooling shadows over
the sundrenched lanes crowded with bargain hunters who wander
through endless displays of tropical fruits and vegetables, kitchen-
ware and antiques - literally a shopper's paradise.

CARMEL MARKET, Tel Aviv

105

The Levites with instruments of music of the Lord, which David the King had made to praise the Lord,... and the priests sounded trumpets before them, and all Israel stood.

Chronicles 7

The Mann Auditorium, Tel Aviv

MANN AUDITORIUM - Tel Aviv

Tel Aviv can rightfully be proud of Mann Auditorium, the largest concert hall in Israel. Its superb accoustics satisfy the expectations of a nation of music lovers who attend in shirtsleeves and leave "standing room only" for every performance. Isaac Stern and other internationally known artists consider it their home away from home. Permanent headquarters for the Israel Philharmonic Orchestra, it stands adjacent to the Helena Rubenstein Pavilion, with which it forms the Tel Aviv Cultural Center.

The flowers
appear on the earth,
The time of singing has
come, and the voice of
the turtle dove is heard
in our land. The fig tree
puts forth her fruit,
and the grape vines are
in blossom, they give forth
fragrance. Arise my
love, my fair one and
come away

Song of Solomon

HELENA RUBINSTEIN MEMORIAL GARDEN
When the citizens of Tel Aviv honored the memory of the founder of Israel's cosmetic industry they could not have created a more fitting memorial than an ever-flowering monument, the garden named after her. Adjacent is Tel Aviv's most important Art Museum, The Helena Rubinstein Pavilion of Contemporary Art, showing the works of local and foreign artists.

הגן ליד המר, רזאון על שם הלנה רוב־כשטיין

HELENA RUBENSTEIN MEMORIAL GARDEN
TEL AVIV

Alex Stern

Except the Lord
build the house,
they labour in
vain that build it:
Except the Lord
keep the city, the watch-
man waketh but in vain.

psalm 127

DIZENGOFF CIRCLE,
TEL AVIV

117

DIZENGOFF CIRCLE Tel Aviv

In 1909 a group of determined pioneers set their shovels into a sand dune on the shore of the Mediterranean and declared, "Here shall be built the city of Tel Aviv." Among them was Meir Dizengoff, who became the city's first mayor and for whom the street and circle were named. On hot summer days laughing children splash in the pool at the circle's center while elderly citizens on nearby benches smile and relive their childhood. And at any time of the year at night, multitudes of gay tourists and Israelis stroll past its numerous sidewalk cafes and enjoy its international cuisine.

Solomon decided to build a house for the name of the Lord ✦ "Now therefore send me a man skillful to work in gold, and in silver, and in brass, and in iron, and in purple, and crimson and blue" ... "...and we will take wood out of Lebanon as much as thou shalt need; and we will bring it to thee in floats by sea to Joppa; and thou shall carry it up to Jerusalem".

Chronicles 1

JAFFA

According to the Old Testament, ancient 'Jappa' was founded after the flood and was named for Japheth, the son of Noah. Archaic Egyptian records indicate the existance of 'Jappa' before the twelve tribes entered Canaan. The ancient structures now used as artists' studios and night clubs are a great attraction to tourists and Israelis.

A STREET IN OLD JAFFA ~ ISRAEL

My people shall
dwell in peaceable
habitations and in sure
dwellings, and in quiet
resting places;

Isaiah 32

A SCENE IN BETHLEHEM

A SCENE IN BETHLEHEM
The biblical theme, Peace on Earth Goodwill-Towards Man, is personified by this group of three citizens in the ancient town of Bethlehem. Although their attire indicates diverse backgrounds the harmony between them as they sit relaxed on the fallen Roman Column is quite apparent.

As I live saith the King whose name is the Lord of hosts, Surely as Tabor is among the mountains and as Car-mel by the sea, so shall He cometh.

Jeremiah 46

CRUSADER ARCH

The Crusader Arch stands among the antiquities at the summit of Mt. Tabor, not far from the Church of the Transfiguration. It intrigued the artist enough to stop and sketch it. At the base of this prominent mountain lies the great Valley of Jezreel, a region rich in Biblical memories, including the battle of the tribes under Deborah against the Cananites and the stand of Josephus Flavius against the Romans.

The Crusader Arch

129

The earth is the Lord's and fullness thereof;
The world and they that dwell within. For he hath founded it upon the seas, and established it upon the floods.

Who shall ascend into the mountain of the Lord? Who shall stand in His Holy place?

A Psalm of David 24

עמקים בנגב
VALLEYS IN THE NEGEV, Israel

Alu Stern

133

THE NEGEV - meaning South
Over half of tiny Israel is awe-inspiring desert rich in biblical
history. Exodus relates that after leaving Egypt the Hebrews wan-
dered through the Negev on their way to Canaan, the Promised
Land. The Negev has finally awakened from its deep sleep and
after centuries of neglect is responding to the efforts of hard working
pioneers in agriculture, mining and other industries.

And after six days
Jesus taketh
Peter, James
and John his brother
and taketh them up into
a high mountain apart.
And was transfigured
before them: and His
face did shine like the
sun ~~~

Matthew 17

CHURCH OF THE TRANSFIGURATION

From earliest Christian times Mt. Tabor has been believed to be the scene of the Transfiguration. The present Franciscan bascilica was built in 1921 - 3 over the ruins of sixth and twelfth century Bzyantine and Crusader churches that were destroyed in 1262. It holds three chaples, one each for Jesus, Moses and Elias. His Holiness Paul VI prayed here in 1964.

CHURCH OF THE TRANSFIGURATION
MT. TABOR, ISRAEL

137

A land whose
stones are iron,
and out of whose
hills thou mayest dig
brass ⸻

Deuteronomy 8

KING SOLOMON'S MINES.

PILLARS OF KING SOLOMON'S MINES - The Negev
A portion of the text in Deuteronomy led to the discovery in 1950
of the remains of King Solomon's copper mines when the renouned
Rabbi Nelson Glick located primitive furnaces near Timna. Pottery
found in the area was determined to be of King Solomon's period.
Today the mines are again commercially productive.

Joseph took the body of Jesus ... and laid it in a sepulchre which he had carved out of rock ... And the Angel said to the women ... go quickly and tell his disciples, He has risen from the dead.

St. Matthew

THE HOLY SEPULCHRE

The body of Christ lies in a sepulchre sheltered within the Crusader-built Church of the Holy Sepulchre in the Christian Quarter of old Jerusalem. This holiest shrine in Christiandom contains chapels of various denominations, including the Franciscan, Greek, Georgian, Copt and Armenian. Ownership of the church is claimed, however, by only the Catholic, Greek and Armenian communities.

COURTYARD OF
THE HOLY SEPULCHRE

145

Lo, thou art unto them as a very lovely song of one that hath a pleasant voice and play well on an instrument.

Ezekiel 34

Roman Theater, Caesarea

149

THE ROMAN AMPHITHEATRE

The Port of Caesarea was built by King Herod the Great about twenty-two B.C. and was the capitol of the Romans in Palestine for five hundred years. The amphitheatre, only a part of what remains of the port, was constructed in the second century and its ruins partially restored in the nineteen sixties. This dramatic site comes to life again when special events such as Israel Philharmonic concerts, international competition and Biblical productions take place here.

To be a Baha'í It simply means to love all the world to love humanity and try to serve it to work for universal peace and universal brotherhood

Abdu'l-Baha'

THE BAHA'I SHRINE OF THE BAB'
The Holy Land has been the International Center of the New World
Religion, the Baha'i Faith, since 1868, when Bah'v'llah its founder,
was exiled to Akka. The shrine is constructed of Chiampo marble and
rose granite. Its golden dome atop Mt. Carmel is visible from miles
away, and visitors to its exquisite formal garden can view the whole
of Haifa and the Mediterranean coast.

BAHAI TEMPLE
HAIFA,

153

For from olden
times we have
undertaken to
serve neither the Romans
nor any other lords,
except God only, for
only He rules over man
in truth and in justice.

From-Gl'azar's oration
Josephus Flavious, Jewish War

MASADA

MASSADA

Nineteen hundred years ago on the edge of the Dead Sea a most dramatic event in Jewish history took place. Here for three years 967 men, women and children held off 10,000 Roman Legionnaires in the last Jewish resistance against Rome. The Romans eventually constructed a ramp to the mountain top and broke through the embattlements but found an empty victory, for with the exception of two women and five children, the defendants had taken their own lives.

The acts of
Hezekiah, and
all his might, and
how he made a~~~
conduit, and carried
water into the city,
are they not written
in the Chronicles of
the Kings of Judah?

II Kings

ROMAN AQUEDUCT OF CAESAREA

The ruins of the high-level aqueduct of Caesarea remain a classic example of the great engineering skill of the Romans of the second century. This aqueduct conducted water from mountain springs to the Roman capitol of the region for nearly a thousand years.

ROMAN AQUADUCT, Caesarea

Then the Lord rained upon Sodom and upon Go·morrah brimstone and fire ... and He overthrew these cities and all the plain, and all the inhabitants of the cities and that which grew upon the ground.

Genesis 6

ROMAN ENCAMPMENTS and
the DEAD SEA from MASSADA

THE DEAD SEA from MASSADA

From their refuge high atop Massada and protected by their encase-
ments, Masada's heroic defenders looked down upon the peaceful
waters of the Dead Sea. Its serenity was belied, however, by the
powerful Roman Legions encircled about the mountain fortress.
Roman seige walls and campsites are still standing today.

On following pages

ACKNOWLEDGMENTS

To JOHN PREYER, Calligrapher—a most appreciative 'thank you' for his excellent handiwork and patience, understanding and friendship. His talented calligraphy throughout the book has enhanced it beautifully.

To STEVEN BERRETTA, my friend and printer—and an artist in his own right—my thanks for his devotion and fine craftsmanship displayed in the printing of the book, and for his companionship during the many long days and nights of work.

To MIMI GAUSS, my daughter—a father's affectionate embrace and thanks for her sensitive editing and constructive criticism often suggested throughout the planning and production of this book.

Alec Stern

THE ARTIST

Alec Stern has achieved renown as an etcher and illustrator, but he is a printer, engraver, musician, philosopher—and a lover of the land of Israel.

Born of immigrant Jewish parents in 1904, his earliest memories are of tall, white sailing ships emerging through the fog of San Francisco's Golden Gate. His early memories of vistas from that city's hills have carried over to an affinity for the port of Haifa, so often compared to his native city.

The artist's creative talent revealed itself early in life when, prevented by a leg injury from joining in school sports, he would remain at his desk trying to master the art of drawing, then a challenge for him. By the time he was 12 he was unofficial art instructor to his class and later, while on a four-year scholarship at the California School of Fine Arts, he found himself teaching his old grammar school instructor. Another year at Columbia University earned him his teaching credential.

continued

After four years of "bread-and-butter" jobs with printers, advertising agencies, and art studios he secured a job with the San Francisco Chronicle, where his drawings of maritime subjects were featured for three years. In 1935, he was sent on a cruise to New York by his newspaper and the Grace Line to create etchings of the various ports of call. The trip paid an unexpected dividend, for the passengers, including Mrs. Theodore Roosevelt, began buying his work.

Magnetized by the turbulent crowds, creaking pushcarts and clattering "El" of New York, he stayed on and freelanced his talents to publishing companies. Here he met his wife, Anne, a buyer of artwork who became his most fastidious critic.

The arrival of their son, Leonard, in 1939 necessitated increased income, so the artist became a designer for a large company while continuing to produce greeting cards and etchings for a clientele he had developed by phoning New York firms alphabetically from the telephone book. ("My list of clients never got beyond 'A,' so successful were the results.")

In 1942, while the government was using Stern's artistic skills to produce animated military training films, their daughter, Mimi, was born.

After the war, the Sterns returned to San Francisco, where the artist became his own publisher. His self-built etching press and new lithographic equipment were the foundation of his present fully-equipped printing plant.

Despite the enormous range of operation in his extremely successful one-man business, every facet of the artist's work bears the stamp of a master. "I am more critical of my work than my clients are," he says. The challenge of combining lithography with etchings has been the ideal compromise between Stern's creative urge and mechanical abilities as etcher, printer, cameraman, and platemaker.

The diversity of his clients ranges from nationally known companies to civic and cultural organizations and several foreign governments.

He first visited Israel in 1966. Experiences such as a desert tour through the very canyons travelled by the ancient Hebrews in attacking Egyptian forces, the same route that David Ben Gurion's biblical studies showed might again be used to surprise the Egyptians during the Israeli War of Independence, put Stern in intimate touch with the history of his people and with modern-day Israel.

In 1971, he returned with an economic study group. By this time, the artist's etchings of Israel were well known, and Jerusalem's Mayor Teddy Kolleck presented the Jerusalem Museum with two prints for its permanent collection.

Today, at the age of 70, the artist still works 12 to 16 hour days, often drawing long into the night, when all is quiet and he can concentrate. His reputation is now so great that people from all parts of America call to see him at his studio. There are two reasons for these visits: to learn how such beautiful work can be produced in such great profusion, and to learn more about the man behind the drawing board.

The artist declares: "Sincerity is reflected in an artist's work, while shallowness produces a shallow art."

Certainly the depth and sincerity of his interest in Israel, the Land of the Bible, is reflected here in his book.

THE STUDIO

Starting with a drawing board and an etching press built by the artist as a student, the studio in San Mateo, California, grew from a small, converted barn into a large, skylighted, ivy-covered structure. With the gradual acquisition of a full-fledged printing plant equipped with a camera and darkroom, platemaking equipment, a variety of presses, and bindery department, Alec Stern needed to acquire new skills. In addition to an artist's beret, he wears the hats of a cameraman, platemaker, bindery man, and pressman.

A nationwide clientele of individuals and business firms has used his etchings as gifts and greeting cards for over 40 years.

Visitors from all parts of the world drop in to view the display of his large collection of prints and the operation of this unique studio. Here they find such diversified themes as the artist's favorite American cities, ships, historical subjects, animals and national parks.

All subjects are also available as etched greeting cards for personal or business use.

ALEC STERN STUDIO / 150 NORTH B STREET
SAN MATEO, CALIFORNIA 94401

THE BOOK

THIS BOOK WAS DESIGNED BY AND PRODUCED IN THE STUDIO OF ALEC STERN BY LITHOGRAPHY ON AN ATF 22 PRESS OF THE '40's VINTAGE.

THE ETCHINGS:	Reproduced from the original drawings and lithographs by Alec Stern
THE SCRIPTURES:	Selected by Alec Stern
CALLIGRAPHY:	John Preyer
DESCRIPTIVE TEXT:	Alec Stern
EDITING:	Miriam Gauss
COMPOSITION FOR DESCRIPTIVE TEXT:	Studio of Alec Stern
COMPOSITION FOR BALANCE OF BOOK:	Mackenzie & Harris, Inc., San Francisco
PORTRAIT OF ARTIST:	Anthony Deauford
PRESSWORK:	Steven Barretta
HALFTONES (150 line screen) AND PLATES:	Produced by Studio of Alec Stern
TYPE FACES:	Arrighi and Centaur
PAPER:	175 lb. Andorra Text
BINDING:	Stecher-Traung-Schmidt, San Francisco

ISRAELS

PROTECTION OF HOLY PLACES LAW 5727-1967

Adopted by the Knesset (Parliament) on 27 June 1967.

1. The Holy Places shall be protected from desecration and any other violation and from anything likely to violate the freedom of access of the members of the various religions to the places sacred to them or their feelings with regard to those places.

2. (a) Whoever desecrates or otherwise violates a Holy Place shall be liable to imprisonment for a term of seven years.

   (b) Whoever does anything that is likely to violate the freedom of access of the members of the various religions to the places sacred to them or their feelings with regard to those places shall be liable to imprisonment for a term of five years.

3. This law shall add to and not derogate from any other law.

4. The Minister of Religious Affairs is charged with the implementation of this law and he may, after consultation with or upon the proposal of representatives of the religions concerned, and with the consent of the Minister of Justice, make regulations as to any matter relating to such implementation.

5. This law shall come into force on the date of its adoption by the Knesset.

LEVI ESHKOL
Prime Minister

ZERAH WAHRHAFTIG
Minister of Religious Affairs

SHNEOR ZALMAN SHAZAR
President